A Visit to CUBA

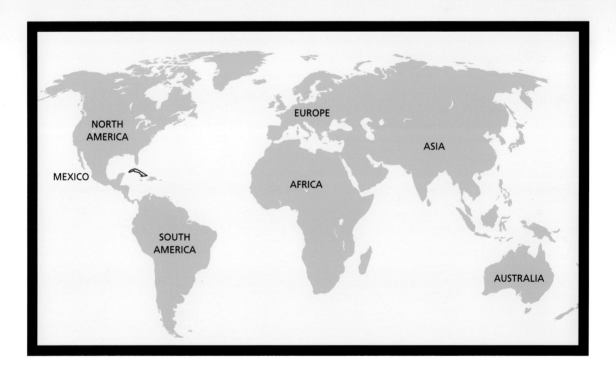

NORTH AMERICA

MEXICO

SOUTH AMERICA

EUROPE

AFRICA

ASIA

AUSTRALIA

Alta Schreier

Heinemann Library
Chicago, Illinois

© 2001 Reed Educational & Professional Publishing
Published by Heinemann Library,
an imprint of Reed Educational & Professional Publishing,
100 N. LaSalle, Suite 1010
Chicago, IL 60602
Customer Service 888-454-2279
Visit our website at www.heinemannlibrary.com

Designed by Ann Tomasic
Printed in Hong Kong

05 04 03 02 01
10 9 8 7 6 5 4 3 2 1

Library of Congress Cataloging-in-Publication Data

Schreier, Alta, 1950-
    Cuba / Alta Schreier.
        p.cm. – (A visit to)
    Includes bibliographical references and index.
    Summary: An introduction to the land, culture, and people of Cuba.
    ISBN 1-57572-380-8 (library binding)
    1. Cuba—Description and travel—Juvenile literature. [1. Cuba.] I. Title. II. Series.

F1765.3 .G55 2000
972.91—dc21

                                        00-029547

Acknowledgments
The publishers would like to thank the following for permission to reproduce photographs:
Corbis/Jeremy Horner, pp. 5, 8, 10, 13, 14; Corbis/Richard Bickel, pp. 6, 11, 19, 20; Corbis/Bill Gentile, pp. 16, 17, 22; Corbis/Tim Page, pp. 18, 25; Corbis/Jan Butchofsky-Houser, p. 15, 29; Corbis/Jon Spaull, p. 21; Corbis/Owen Franken, p. 23; Corbis/Wally McNamee, p. 24; Corbis/Robert van cer Hilst, p. 27; Corbis/Daniel Laine, pp. 26, 28; Eye Ubiquitous/Corbis/James Davis, p. 9; Aurora/PictureQuest/Jose Azel, p. 7; Magnum/PictureQuest/Thomas Hoepker, p. 12

Cover photograph reproduced with permission of Corbis/Bill Gentile.

Every effort has been made to contact copyright holders of any material reproduced in this book. Any omissions will be rectified in subsequent printings if notice is given to the publisher.

Some words are shown in bold, **like this.** You can find out what they mean by looking in the glossary.

Contents

Cuba 4

Land 6

Landmarks 8

Homes 10

Food 12

Clothes 14

Work 16

Transportation 18

Language 20

School 22

Free Time 24

Celebrations 26

The Arts 28

Fact File 30

Glossary 31

Index and More Books to Read 32

Cuba

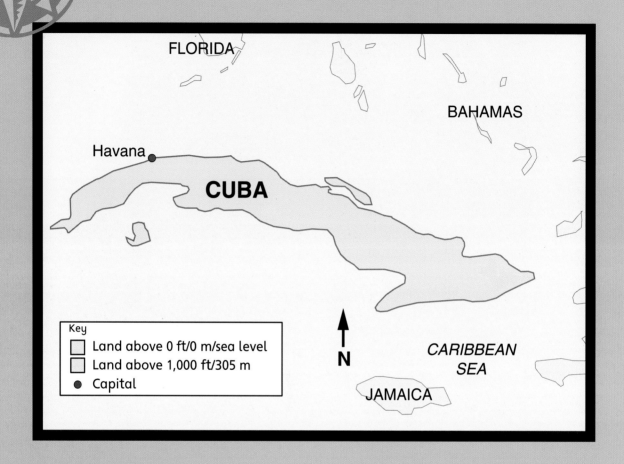

Key
- Land above 0 ft/0 m/sea level
- Land above 1,000 ft/305 m
- Capital

FLORIDA

BAHAMAS

Havana

CUBA

CARIBBEAN SEA

JAMAICA

N

Cuba is a country in the **Caribbean Sea,** south of Florida. It is one big island with some smaller ones nearby.

People in Cuba eat, work, and go to school like you do. Life in Cuba is also **unique**.

Land

Cuba has flat **plains** that are used for farmland. There are also sandy beaches and **coral reefs**. The weather in Cuba is very warm.

There are mountains in Cuba, too. The mountains are covered with forests.

Landmarks

The **capital** of Cuba is Havana. The Capitol building in Havana looks like the United States Capitol building in Washington, D.C.

Morro Castle is an old fort. It was built by people from Spain. It was used 400 years ago to **protect** Havana from pirates.

Homes

Most Cubans live in cities. The cities are crowded, so many people live in apartment buildings. There are some beautiful old buildings. There are new buildings, too.

Most homes in the country are simple.
Some are made of wood from **palm** trees.
They have roofs of palm leaves or grasses.

Food

White rice is the most common food in Cuba. Sometimes it is mixed with black beans. Chicken with rice is popular, too.

Many kinds of fruits grow in Cuba. Bananas, pineapples, oranges, and mangoes are favorites. **Yucca** is a plant that people eat as a vegetable.

Clothes

Cubans dress to keep cool in the hot weather. Many children wear shorts and T-shirts.

For special festivals, men wear white pants and white shirts. Women wear colorful ruffled dresses.

Work

Some Cubans work in factories that make cigars or sugar. There are also factories where people make cloth, shoes, paper, and farm tools.

In the country, there are large farms. The workers there grow **sugarcane** and tobacco. There are also farms for vegetables, such as lettuce, onions, and carrots.

Transportation

There are not many cars in Cuba. In the cities, some people drive old cars from the United States. Most Cubans travel by bus.

On country roads, people use animals to pull wagons. Animals are also used to help farmers in their fields.

Language

Most people in Cuba speak Spanish. This is because Cuba was **settled** by people from Spain.

Spanish uses some of the same letters as English. There are also some extra letters in the Spanish alphabet.

School

Cuban children go to school between the ages of five and fourteen. They wear uniforms to school. There are different colored uniforms for different ages.

In school, children learn math, reading, and history. All schoolchildren do some kind of work during their school day. Some children work in gardens. Older children may work in factories.

Free Time

Baseball is Cuba's national sport. Cuba won the gold medal in baseball in the 1996 Olympic Games.

Cuba's beaches are good for swimming and boating. People like to dive and fish. There are also rowboat and sailboat races.

Celebrations

Cuba's biggest celebration is called Carnival. It is held on July 26. People dance and sing at this festival.

Some people who **settled** in Cuba were
Roman Catholics. Other people who
lived in Cuba were from Africa. So some
Cuban celebrations mix African and
Catholic beliefs.

The Arts

Cuban music mixes sounds from Africa and Spain. Musicians use guitars, drums, and **gourds** to make music and a beat. Dances from Cuba are popular around the world.

In one valley in Cuba, there are large, colorful paintings on some rocks. Inside the rocks are caves. The caves have paintings made by people who lived in Cuba about 1,000 years ago.

Fact File

Name	The Republic of Cuba is the country's full name.
Capital	Cuba's capital is Havana.
Language	The people speak Spanish.
Population	There are about eleven million people living in Cuba.
Money	Cuban money is called the peso.
Religion	Many Cubans are Roman Catholics, but West African beliefs are important.
Products	Sugar is Cuba's most important product, but tobacco and a metal called nickel are also sent to other countries.

Words You Can Learn

hola (OH-la)	hello
adiós (ah-dee-OS)	goodbye
sí (see)	yes
no (no)	no
gracias (GRAH-see-ahs)	thank you
por favor (pore fah-VOR)	please
uno/una (un-oh, un-ah)	one
dos (dohs)	two
tres (trays)	three

Glossary

capital   important city where the government is based

Caribbean Sea   sea south of Florida that is part of the Atlantic Ocean and that is near Central and South America

coral reef   colorful underwater ridge made of the skeletons of small animals called corals

gourd   large fruit with a hard shell that can be dried to make cups, bowls, or musical instruments

Olympic Games international sports competition held every four years

palm   tree without branches that has large leaves at the top and that grows well in warm places

plains   flat land often covered in grass or small bushes that is used for farming

protect   to keep safe

settled   moved from one country to live in another country

sugarcane   kind of tall grass that can be made into sugar

unique   different in a special way

yucca   green plant with stiff leaves that are shaped like swords

Index

arts 28–29

baseball 24

beaches 6, 25

Caribbean Sea 4

Carnival 26

celebrations 26–27

cigars 16, 30

clothes 14–15, 22

crops 17, 30

dance 26, 28

festivals 15, 26–27

Florida 4

food 12–13

forests 7

Havana 8–9, 30

homes 10–11

landmarks 8–9

mountains 7

music 28

Olympic Games 24

Roman Catholic 27, 30

school 22–23

Spanish 20–21, 30

sports 24–25

sugar 16, 30

sugarcane 17

transportation 18–19

United States 4, 8, 18

weather 6

More Books to Read

Dahl, Michael S. *Cuba*. Danbury, Conn.: Children's Press, 1998.

Mara, William P. *Cuba*. Mankato, Minn.: Capstone Press, Inc., 1998.

Staub, Frank J. *Children of Cuba*. Minneapolis: Lerner Publishing Group, 1996. An older reader can help you with this book.